Quilt Art 2005

ENGAGEMENT CALENDAR

A collection of prizewinning
quilts from across the country

Quilts researched and selected by Klaudeen Hansen and Annette Baker

Color photography by Charles R. Lynch, Paducah, KY
and Richard Walker, Schenevus, NY

On the cover:

STAR PLUVIUM by Mary Kay Price, Hinsdale, IL, 69" x 69". After Mary Kay decided her Lone Star looked like a flower, the rest of this original design just followed. She used machine piecing, machine appliqué, and machine quilting. Reverse appliqué was also used to enhance the design. A winner at Quilter's Hall of Fame, Marion, IN, and Pacific International Quilt Festival, Santa Clara, CA.

December/January

MONDAY
27

TUESDAY
28

WEDNESDAY
29

THURSDAY
30

FRIDAY
31

SATURDAY NEW YEAR'S DAY
1

RESCUED TREASURES
by Glenda Goetz, Wheatland, WY, 81" x 92". Scraps rescued from a neighbor's move were used to create 3,360 different pieces needed to make the Y2K quilt pattern. Machine pieced onto a muslin foundation and machine quilted by Audrey Vossler, the friend who originally provided the scraps. Glenda cut the strips, put them into a basket, and randomly drew them out of the basket to position them in the quilt. Displayed at Quilt Wyoming, Douglas, WY.

Features Y2K Quilt pattern by Carol Doak, ©2000.

SUNDAY
2

JANUARY						
S	M	T	W	T	F	S
						1
2	3	4	5	6	7	8
9	10	11	12	13	14	15
16	17	18	19	20	21	22
23	24	25	26	27	28	29
30	31					

JANUARY

MONDAY
3

TUESDAY
4

WEDNESDAY
5

THURSDAY
6

FRIDAY
7

SATURDAY
8

SUNDAY
9

SECOND-HAND ROSE
by Carol Elrod, Indianapolis, IN, 34"
x 39". Carol challenged herself to use
all recycled fabric – either from
Goodwill purchases or castoff pieces
from friends. She was the model and
her husband took the picture used
for construction. She used machine
appliqué, thread painting, fabric
paint, and dye sticks to bring Rose to
life. Displayed at Wholly Rags recycled art exhibit, Sullivan Museum,
Zionsville, IN; Pennsylvania National Quilt Extravaganza and Pacific
International Quilt Festival.

			JANUARY			
S	M	T	W	T	F	S
						1
2	3	4	5	6	7	8
9	10	11	12	13	14	15
16	17	18	19	20	21	22
23	24	25	26	27	28	29
30	31					

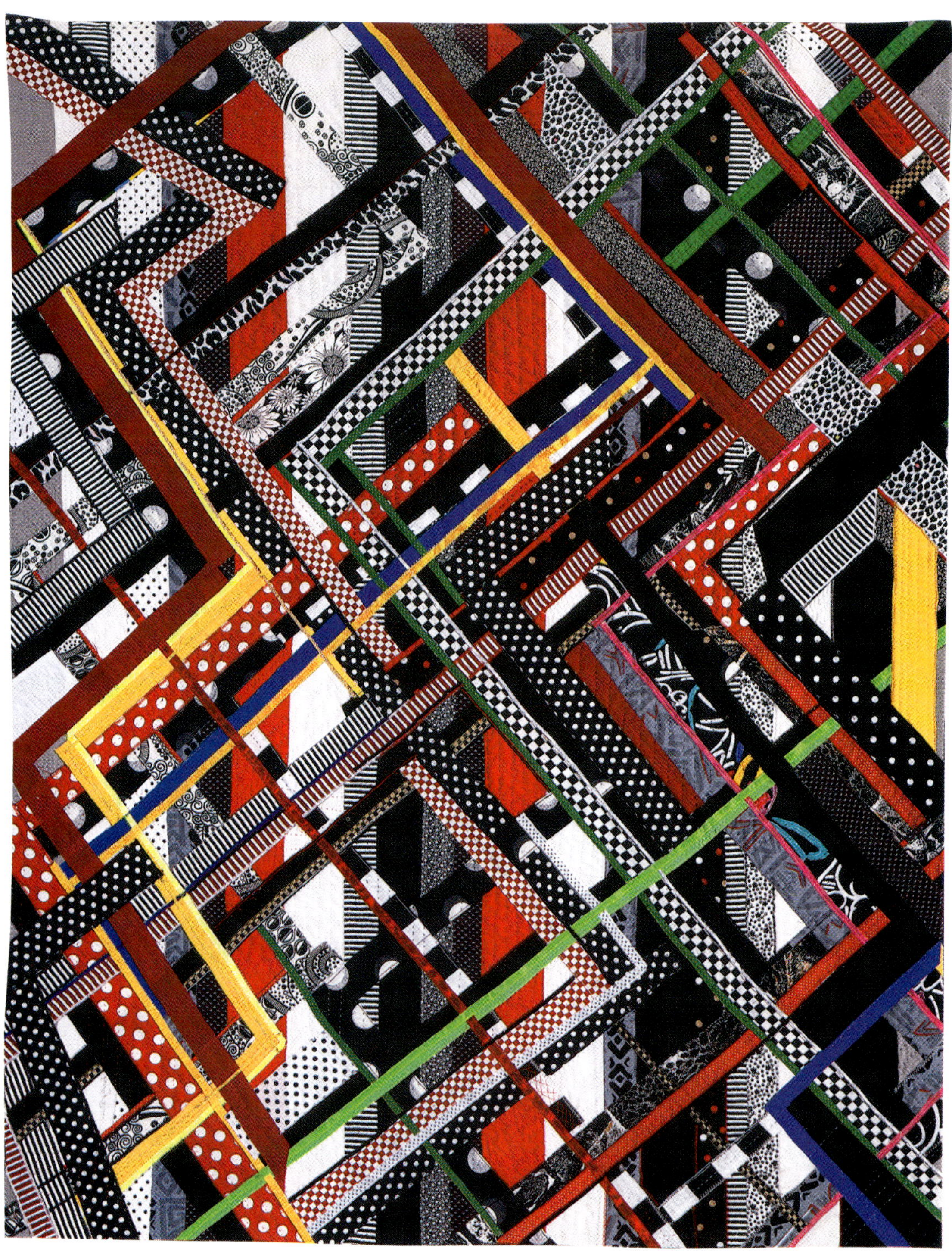

JANUARY

10

11

12

13

14

15

16

CHECK THE PLUMB LINE
by Dorothy Flynn, Columbus, OH, 41" x 52". Dorothy was working "collage style" (placing strips on base fabric with machine appliqué) and wanted to stretch the design by coordinating as many fabrics and colors as possible. She carried the design through the piece so the eye would travel from side to side, always finding something new to see. A winner at the Columbus Cultural Art Center and displayed at the Winter Fair Show, Pols, OH, and at the Dairy Barn, Athens, OH.

			JANUARY			
S	M	T	W	T	F	S
						1
2	3	4	5	6	7	8
9	10	11	12	13	14	15
16	17	18	19	20	21	22
23	24	25	26	27	28	29
30	31					

JANUARY

MONDAY
17

TUESDAY
18

WEDNESDAY
19

THURSDAY
20

FRIDAY
21

SATURDAY
22

SUNDAY
23

PERSIAN STAR
by Nancy Rink, Bakersfield, CA, 93" x 93". An innovative setting for a traditional star, it was hand pieced, appliquéd, embroidered, and hand quilted. The colors and fabrics were taken from the Jinny Beyer Bordering on Brilliance Contest where it was a winner. It was also a winner at Cotton Patch Quilt Show and Best of the Valley Quilt Show. It was displayed at Mid Atlantic Quilt Festival, Williamsburg, VA.

JANUARY

S	M	T	W	T	F	S
						1
2	3	4	5	6	7	8
9	10	11	12	13	14	15
16	17	18	19	20	21	22
23	24	25	26	27	28	29
30	31					

JANUARY

24

25

26

27

28

29

30

YOUNG WINTER
by Sue Soetenga, Eagle River, WI, 48" x 58". Peaceful and quiet, yet glowing, is this original landscape. The background was sketched and divided into 180 curved templates. Cotton, silk, polyester, and blends were used. Some fabrics were "home-dyed" and bound in velvet. The quilting defines and lends texture to nature's elements. The trees are constructed of 62 templates, pieced and applied with needle-turn appliqué. A Best of Show winner at the Trees for Tomorrow Quilt Show, Eagle River, WI.

JANUARY

S	M	T	W	T	F	S
						1
2	3	4	5	6	7	8
9	10	11	12	13	14	15
16	17	18	19	20	21	22
23	24	25	26	27	28	29
30	31					

January/February

MONDAY
31

TUESDAY
1

WEDNESDAY GROUNDHOG DAY
2

THURSDAY
3

FRIDAY
4

SATURDAY
5

SUNDAY
6

STAR WITHIN A STAR by Wendy Butler Berns, Lake Mills, WI, hand quilted by Robynn Van Horne, and owned by Mary Jo Bolan, Hinsdale, IL, 90" x 97". Paper piecing, appliqué, painted fabric, and embellishments create the base for this striking, asymmetrical design. Its surface is enhanced with hand quilting done with metallic and hand-dyed cotton threads. This opportunity quilt was created by Wendy and Robynn and the 65 members of the Salt Creek Quilt Guild. Displayed at AQS, Paducah, KY.

		FEBRUARY				
S	M	T	W	T	F	S
		1	2	3	4	5
6	7	8	9	10	11	12
13	14	15	16	17	18	19
20	21	22	23	24	25	26
27	28					

FEBRUARY

MONDAY
7

TUESDAY
8

WEDNESDAY
9

THURSDAY
10

FRIDAY
11

SATURDAY
12

SUNDAY
13

WANT 2 NECK?
by Shelli Ricci, Apple Valley, MN, quilted by Kim Brunner, 40" x 50". Winning first place after entering her first quilt show is what Shelli did with these romantic creatures. Many techniques including dimensional piecing, beadwork, machine piecing and quilting, and appliqué were used to create this whimsical piece. Shelli also gives credit to a class with Ruth McDowell on how to translate a drawing into fabric. A winner at Treasures of Tomorrow Quilt Show, Marshfield, WI.

FEBRUARY

S	M	T	W	T	F	S
		1	2	3	4	5
6	7	8	9	10	11	12
13	14	15	16	17	18	19
20	21	22	23	24	25	26
27	28					

FEBRUARY

MONDAY　　VALENTINE'S DAY
14

TUESDAY
15

WEDNESDAY
16

THURSDAY
17

FRIDAY
18

SATURDAY
19

SUNDAY
20

COMPASS IN A STORM
by Mary L. Matton, Davidsonville, MD, 80" x 90". Machine pieced and hand quilted. A winner at the Southern Maryland Quilt and Needlework Show and the Annapolis Quilt Guild Show. Also displayed at NQA, Columbus, OH.

Inspired by the Mariner's Compass pattern from *Mariner's Compass Quilts: New Directions* by Judy Mathieson, C&T Publishing, ©1996 and a border pattern from the House of White Birches' book *Pieced Border Collection*, designs by Denyse Saint Arroman, edited by Sandra L. Hatch, ©1996.

FEBRUARY						
S	M	T	W	T	F	S
		1	2	3	4	5
6	7	8	9	10	11	12
13	14	15	16	17	18	19
20	21	22	23	24	25	26
27	28					

FEBRUARY

MONDAY
21

TUESDAY
22

WEDNESDAY
23

THURSDAY
24

FRIDAY
25

SATURDAY
26

LOVE APPLE MAZE
by Johnnie Meeks, Blackhawk, SD, 90" x 94". Johnnie's blocks were machine sewn and inspired by a tiny picture in a magazine. She then pieced together a "canvas" for her floral appliqué blocks and borders – which were all done by hand. The longarm machine quilting was done by Kathy Dahme. A Best of Show and Viewer's Choice winner at the Black Hills Quilt Show, Rapid City, SD.

SUNDAY
27

FEBRUARY						
S	M	T	W	T	F	S
		1	2	3	4	5
6	7	8	9	10	11	12
13	14	15	16	17	18	19
20	21	22	23	24	25	26
27	28					

FEBRUARY/MARCH

MONDAY
28

TUESDAY
1

WEDNESDAY
2

THURSDAY
3

FRIDAY
4

SATURDAY
5

SUNDAY
6

RUBIK'S CUBE
by Katie Adams, Parkland, FL, 40" x 40". Katie created this cube within a cube using the techniques and inspiration provided by Karen Combs' *Optical Illusions for Quilters, AQS*. It was a part of the Quilt Guild Challenge, A Square in a Square, in Coral Springs, FL. Machine pieced and machine quilted. Juried into the Ultimate Guild Challenge exhibit, AQS Quilt Exposition, Nashville, TN.

Features Harlequin Cube pattern by Karen Combs, *Optical Illusions for Quilters, AQS*, ©1997.

			MARCH			
S	M	T	W	T	F	S
		1	2	3	4	5
6	7	8	9	10	11	12
13	14	15	16	17	18	19
20	21	22	23	24	25	26
27	28	29	30	31		

MARCH

TUESDAY
8

WEDNESDAY
9

THURSDAY
10

FRIDAY
11

SATURDAY
12

CROSSROADS 1879 TO 2003 by Paula E. Mariedaughter, St. Paul, AR, 83" x 100". Inspiration for this piece came from a ca. 1879 quilt top by Beck West in the Smithsonian Collection. The quilt top was drafted and constructed by Paula from reproduction fabrics and one batik to bring it into this century. Hand quilted by 30 members of the Q.U.I.L.T. Guild of Northwest Arkansas, Rogers. Displayed at Heirlooms IX, Rogers, AR.

SUNDAY
13

MARCH						
S	M	T	W	T	F	S
		1	2	3	4	5
6	7	8	9	10	11	12
13	14	15	16	17	18	19
20	21	22	23	24	25	26
27	28	29	30	31		

MARCH

MONDAY
14

TUESDAY
15

WEDNESDAY
16

THURSDAY
17

FRIDAY
18

SATURDAY NATIONAL QUILTING DAY
19

FLORAL FANTASY
by Carol A Hodgden, Oxford Jct., IA, 66" x 72". Carol enclosed her rendition of Pat Campbell's Turkish Delight pattern with her own original border inspired by the border on a rug in her home. The appliqué is all done by hand and the quilting is a combination of hand and machine. Displayed at the Eastern Iowa Heirloom Quilter's Show, Cedar Rapids, IA, and a winner at the Dyersville Quilt Show, Dyersville, IA.

Inspired by a Pat Campbell design, ©1996.

SUNDAY PALM SUNDAY
20 SPRING EQUINOX

MARCH						
S	M	T	W	T	F	S
		1	2	3	4	5
6	7	8	9	10	11	12
13	14	15	16	17	18	19
20	21	22	23	24	25	26
27	28	29	30	31		

MARCH

MONDAY
21

TUESDAY
22

WEDNESDAY
23

THURSDAY
24

FRIDAY   GOOD FRIDAY
25

FIESTA
by Louisa L. Smith, Loveland, CO, 37" x 37". This party on a quilt is an original design in a series called "strips 'n curves." It is machine pieced and machine quilted, then beaded and embellished by hand. This work has traveled extensively as part of Louisa's trunk show.

SATURDAY
26

SUNDAY   EASTER SUNDAY
27

			MARCH			
S	M	T	W	T	F	S
		1	2	3	4	5
6	7	8	9	10	11	12
13	14	15	16	17	18	19
20	21	22	23	24	25	26
27	28	29	30	31		

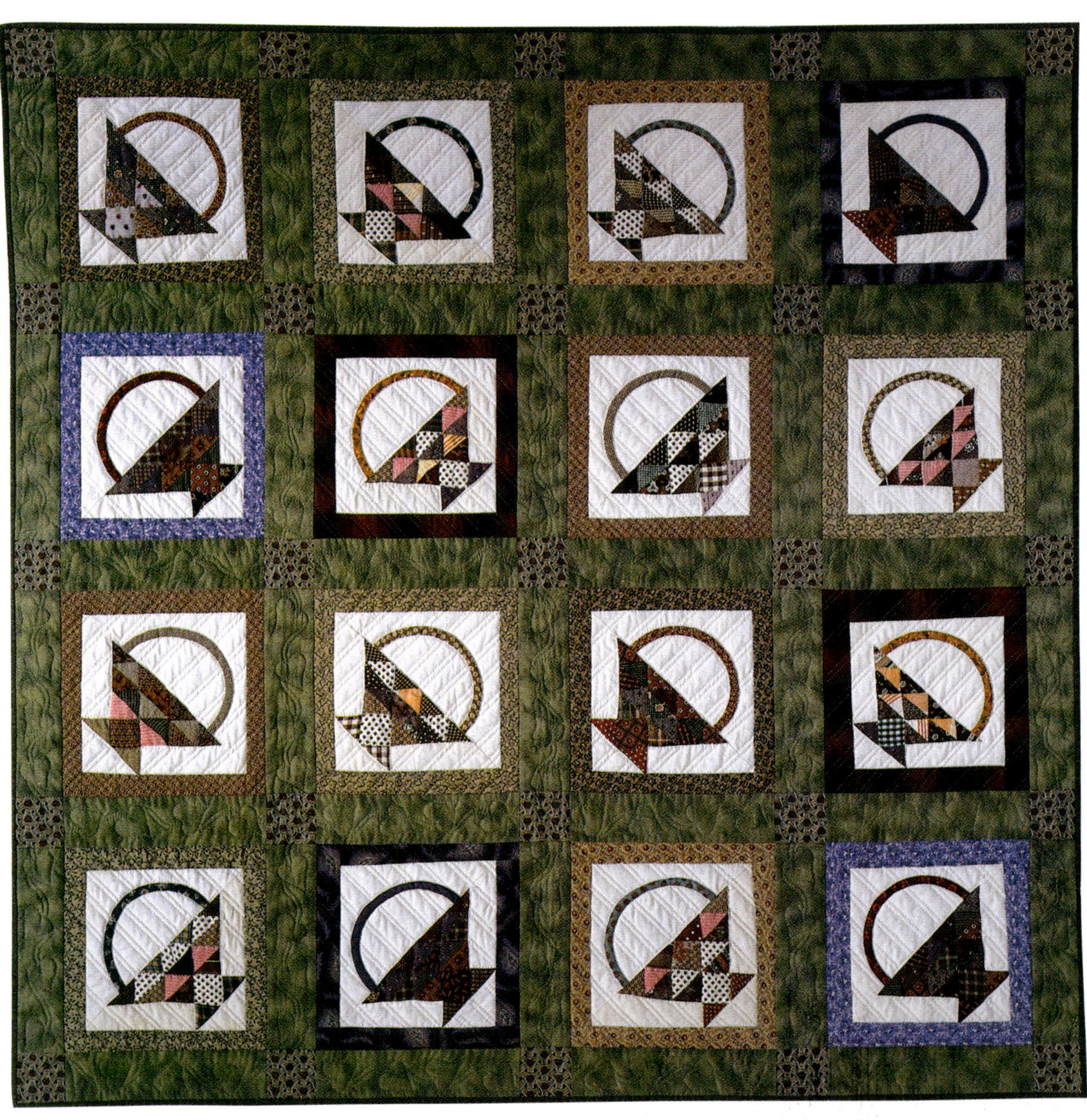

MARCH/APRIL

MONDAY
28

TUESDAY
29

WEDNESDAY
30

THURSDAY
31

FRIDAY   APRIL FOOL'S DAY
1

TRICENTENNIAL
by Didi Salvatierra, Bel Air, MD, 62" x 62". Spanning three centuries, this quilt includes a wonderful selection of fabrics, hand pieced by an unknown 19th century quiltmaker. Didi purchased the incomplete antique basket blocks in the 20th century and completed the piece in the 21st century. Who says we never finish what we start! Hand appliquéd, hand and machine pieced, and hand quilted. Displayed at AQS, Nashville, TN, Flying Geese Quilt Guild Show, MD, and NQA, Columbus, OH.

SATURDAY
2

SUNDAY   DAYLIGHT SAVINGS
3   TIME BEGINS

		APRIL				
S	M	T	W	T	F	S
					1	2
3	4	5	6	7	8	9
10	11	12	13	14	15	16
17	18	19	20	21	22	23
24	25	26	27	28	29	30

APRIL

MONDAY

4

TUESDAY

5

WEDNESDAY

6

THURSDAY

7

FRIDAY

8

SATURDAY

9

SUNDAY

10

TULIPS
by Kay Wilson, Wrightwood, CA, 37" x 50". The drama of black and white sets off Kay's original tulip design. Her flowers were constructed by hand and machine and hand appliquéd to the background. To simulate live flowers, she used paint and bleach, water-color pencils, and colored pens. The leaves were tucked to give them the proper texture. Displayed at the Pacific International Quilt Festival, Road to California, and Pennsylvania National Quilt Extravaganza.

| | | APRIL | | | | |
S	M	T	W	T	F	S
					1	2
3	4	5	6	7	8	9
10	11	12	13	14	15	16
17	18	19	20	21	22	23
24	25	26	27	28	29	30

APRIL

MONDAY
11

TUESDAY
12

WEDNESDAY
13

THURSDAY
14

FRIDAY
15

SATURDAY
16

SUNDAY
17

			APRIL			
S	M	T	W	T	F	S
					1	2
3	4	5	6	7	8	9
10	11	12	13	14	15	16
17	18	19	20	21	22	23
24	25	26	27	28	29	30

APRIL

TUESDAY
19

WEDNESDAY
20

AQS QUILT SHOW & CONTEST, PADUCAH

THURSDAY
21

AQS QUILT SHOW & CONTEST, PADUCAH

FRIDAY
22

AQS QUILT SHOW & CONTEST, PADUCAH

SATURDAY
23

AQS QUILT SHOW & CONTEST, PADUCAH

TUDOR ROMANCE
by Kathy McNeil, Marysville, WA, 66" x 80". To recreate the look of an Old English tapestry, Britain's royal bird, the swan, is featured. Kathy captured the essence of the environment by using hand appliqué, thread play, and painting, as well as machine embroidery and paper piecing. Machine quilting brings texture to the background. It was invited to hang at the International Quilt Show in Barcelona, Spain.

SUNDAY
24

PASSOVER BEGINS

APRIL						
S	M	T	W	T	F	S
					1	2
3	4	5	6	7	8	9
10	11	12	13	14	15	16
17	18	19	20	21	22	23
24	25	26	27	28	29	30

APRIL/MAY

MONDAY
25

TUESDAY
26

WEDNESDAY
27

THURSDAY
28

FRIDAY
29

SATURDAY
30

SUNDAY
1

WINDOWS BY THE RIVER
by Linda Schutz, Carver, MN, 90" x 92". This is an original design by Linda inspired by the historic church by the river in her hometown. The glass in her stained glass windows is created by using strips of water-color fabrics. Machine pieced, appliquéd, and quilted. A Viewer's Choice winner at the Silver Threads Quilt Show and Conference, St. Paul, MN, and at the Chanhassen Quilt Show in Minnesota.

		MAY				
S	M	T	W	T	F	S
1	2	3	4	5	6	7
8	9	10	11	12	13	14
15	16	17	18	19	20	21
22	23	24	25	26	27	28
29	30	31				

 MAY

MONDAY
2

TUESDAY
3

WEDNESDAY
4

THURSDAY
5

FRIDAY
6

SATURDAY
7

SUNDAY   MOTHER'S DAY
8

			MAY			
S	M	T	W	T	F	S
1	2	3	4	5	6	7
8	9	10	11	12	13	14
15	16	17	18	19	20	21
22	23	24	25	26	27	28
29	30	31				

MONDAY
9

TUESDAY
10

WEDNESDAY
11

THURSDAY
12

FRIDAY
13

TIES THAT BIND ©1999
by Betty E. Ives, Windsor, Ontario, Canada, 75" x 87". Swirling ribbons of hand-dyed fabrics purchased in Japan were the source of this original design. Creative use of ribbon floss, Sliver™ and rayon thread, lamé, and hand-dyed rayon fabrics. Machine and hand quilted with machine appliqué. A winner at Mountain Quiltfest, Pigeon Forge, TN; McMinn Museum, Athens, TN; displayed in Ontario at the Windsor Quilter's Guild Show and Erie Shores Quilt Show, Leamington.

SATURDAY
14

SUNDAY
15

			MAY			
S	M	T	W	T	F	S
1	2	3	4	5	6	7
8	9	10	11	12	13	14
15	16	17	18	19	20	21
22	23	24	25	26	27	28
29	30	31				

 MAY

MONDAY
16

TUESDAY
17

WEDNESDAY
18

THURSDAY
19

FRIDAY
20

SATURDAY
21

SUNDAY
22

MAY						
S	M	T	W	T	F	S
1	2	3	4	5	6	7
8	9	10	11	12	13	14
15	16	17	18	19	20	21
22	23	24	25	26	27	28
29	30	31				

MONDAY
23

TUESDAY
24

WEDNESDAY
25

THURSDAY
26

FRIDAY
27

DANDELIONS
by Tone Haugen-Cogburn, Maryville, TN, 42" x 42". Several trips to Norway and many photos of the large and hardy dandelions that grow there grew into this wall quilt. A machine-pieced background, raw-edge appliqué with free-motion embroidery, and quilting add texture and depth to this hardy yellow weed.

SATURDAY
28

SUNDAY
29

			MAY			
S	M	T	W	T	F	S
1	2	3	4	5	6	7
8	9	10	11	12	13	14
15	16	17	18	19	20	21
22	23	24	25	26	27	28
29	30	31				

MAY/JUNE

MONDAY
30

TUESDAY
31

WEDNESDAY
1

THURSDAY
2

FRIDAY
3

SATURDAY
4

SUNDAY
5

GRIDBLOCK
by Kent Williams, Madison, WI, 63" x 86". Four colors (green, purple, red, and yellow) play varying roles in this pattern. Kent designed a grid structure and split the squares, strip-piecing one of the half-squares. Colors rotate through four quadrants for a distinct, yet related, look. By rotating individual blocks, Kent created Escher-like shapes out of the stripped pieces, adding depth and complexity. Machine pieced and quilted. Displayed at the Prairie Heritage Quilt Show, Sun Prairie, WI.

			JUNE			
S	M	T	W	T	F	S
			1	2	3	4
5	6	7	8	9	10	11
12	13	14	15	16	17	18
19	20	21	22	23	24	25
26	27	28	29	30		

A Time to Remember

Be the envy of all your friends – Order the 2006 Quilt Art Engagement Calendar now!

Beautiful, magnificent, wonderful, breathtaking...

...are words that can easily describe this best-selling weekly calendar. Once again, Klaudeen Hansen and Annette Baker have traveled the country looking for outstanding quilts that will add to your love of quilting. A brief yet informative description accompanies each quilt. And there is plenty of writing space to help you keep track of all your favorite quilting events.

#6600, 7" x 9", 112 pgs. $12.95

Quilt Art 2006 Engagement Calendar available May 1, 2005.

- Detach and Return -

______	**#6600**	**Quilt Art 2006 Engagement Calendar**	@ $12.95	__________
______	**#6350**	**Quilt Art 2005 Engagement Calendar**	@ $12.95	__________

For more information on becoming a member of AQS, check here ☐ **#1862**

KY residents add 6% sales tax __________

*Postage & Handling __________

TOTAL ENCLOSED __________

Method of Payment

Make checks payable to American Quilter's Society.

I have enclosed a check for $__________ Ck# __________

Charge my: ☐ MasterCard ☐ VISA ☐ DISCOVER NOVUS Exp. ________

Card # ☐☐☐☐☐☐☐☐☐☐☐☐☐☐☐☐

Signature __________________________

Name ______________________________________

Address ___________________________________

City __________________ State ______ Zip __________

Country ___________________________________

***POSTAGE CHARGES**
U.S. customers add $3 for first item and 50¢ for each additional item.
SERVICE ABROAD
Canadian and International orders add $3 per item (minimum 8 week delivery), $5 per item (10–15 business days), or $8 per item (8–10 business days).

American Quilter's Society

P. O. Box 3290 • Paducah, KY 42002-3290
Phone: 270-898-7903 • FAX: 270-898-1173
www.AQSquilt.com • e-mail: info@AQSquilt.com

EC5

JUNE

MONDAY
6

TUESDAY
7

WEDNESDAY
8

THURSDAY
9

FRIDAY
10

SATURDAY
11

SUNDAY
12

POPPIES IN THE GARDEN by Bethanne G. Nemesh, Allentown, PA, 80" x 103". While the design of this quilt is historical, Bethanne chose all the elements including a traditional star and folksy appliqué. Several washings enhance the antique look. Machine piecing, fusible interfacing, turned appliqué, machine appliqué, machine quilting, hand embroidery, and hand stamped fabric were used. Displayed at the Indiana Heritage Quilt Show; NQA, Columbus, OH; Quilt Odyssey, Gettysburg, PA, and Pennsylvania Quilt Extravaganza.

			JUNE			
S	M	T	W	T	F	S
			1	2	3	4
5	6	7	8	9	10	11
12	13	14	15	16	17	18
19	20	21	22	23	24	25
26	27	28	29	30		

JUNE

SWIMMING UP THE RIVER GIVES YOU THE BLUES

by Charla J. Viehe, Olive Branch, MS, 62" x 57". A multitude of beads and other embellishments take these basic traditional blocks to another level. When set on point they take on a "fishy" persona. With colors that remind you of sunlight filtering through water, this quilt was a sure thing for her guild challenge, Blues on the River. Juried into the Ultimate Guild Challenge Exhibit, AQS Quilt Exposition, Nashville, TN.

			JUNE			
S	M	T	W	T	F	S
			1	2	3	4
5	6	7	8	9	10	11
12	13	14	15	16	17	18
19	20	21	22	23	24	25
26	27	28	29	30		

JUNE

MONDAY
20

TUESDAY SUMMER SOLSTICE
21

WEDNESDAY
22

THURSDAY
23

FRIDAY
24

SATURDAY
25

SUNDAY
26

AMONG THE LEAVES
by Karen Labelle, Land O'Lakes, WI, 53" x 70". Karen's recreation of a pattern designed by Cheryl Wittmayer is embellished with hand embroidery to increase surface interest. She used the crayon-coloring technique to color the designs in the blocks. Machine pieced and quilted. Displayed at A Walk in the North Woods Quilt Show, Eagle River, WI.

Features Among the Leaves pattern by Cheryl Wittmayer/Sew Be It ©2000.

			JUNE			
S	M	T	W	T	F	S
			1	2	3	4
5	6	7	8	9	10	11
12	13	14	15	16	17	18
19	20	21	22	23	24	25
26	27	28	29	30		

JUNE/JULY

ROSE GARDEN IN CENTRAL PARK

by Arlene King, Annapolis, MD, 40" x 40". This original design is a delightful combination of inspiration from Katie Pasquini Masopust's work and a special showing of Tumbling Blocks quilts. The "boxes of roses" came together after Arlene saw the rosy challenge fabric. Best of Challenge at the Sun Prairie Heritage Quilt Show, Sun Prairie, WI. Displayed at the Black Hills Quilt Show, Rapid City, SD, and at the Wyoming State Guild Show in Douglas.

JULY

S	M	T	W	T	F	S
					1	2
3	4	5	6	7	8	9
10	11	12	13	14	15	16
17	18	19	20	21	22	23
24	25	26	27	28	29	30
31						

MONDAY INDEPENDENCE DAY

4

TUESDAY

5

WEDNESDAY

6

THURSDAY

7

FRIDAY

8

SATURDAY

9

SUNDAY

10

WORLD ON FIRE
by Tracie Rebsamen, Fayetteville, AR, 65" x 65". A piece of bold striped fabric inspired the color palette for this Lone Star. Some techniques from the Jan Krentz book *Lone Star Quilts & Beyond* were used in construction. Tracie also used machine piecing, paper foundations, appliqué, and machine quilting with variegated jewel tone thread. A prizewinner at the Northwest Arkansas Quilt Guild Show.

Features a variation of the Spiral Lone Star pattern by Jan Krentz, *Lone Star Quilts & Beyond*, C&T Publishing, ©2001.

			JULY			
S	M	T	W	T	F	S
					1	2
3	4	5	6	7	8	9
10	11	12	13	14	15	16
17	18	19	20	21	22	23
24	25	26	27	28	29	30
31						

JULY

MONDAY
11

TUESDAY
12

WEDNESDAY
13

THURSDAY
14

FRIDAY
15

SATURDAY
16

SUNDAY
17

JULY

S	M	T	W	T	F	S
					1	2
3	4	5	6	7	8	9
10	11	12	13	14	15	16
17	18	19	20	21	22	23
24	25	26	27	28	29	30
31						

July

MONDAY
18

TUESDAY
19

WEDNESDAY
20

THURSDAY
21

FRIDAY
22

SATURDAY
23

SUNDAY
24

		JULY				
S	M	T	W	T	F	S
					1	2
3	4	5	6	7	8	9
10	11	12	13	14	15	16
17	18	19	20	21	22	23
24	25	26	27	28	29	30
31						

JULY

MONDAY
25

TUESDAY
26

WEDNESDAY
27

THURSDAY
28

FRIDAY
29

SATURDAY
30

SUNDAY
31

POULET DE FLEUR
by Pat Moore, Punta Gorda, FL, 61" x 73". Second in a series by Pat exploring construction and technique methods for large-scale designs. This oversized chicken was inspired by Maggie Walker's Country Journal pattern. Flowers and leaves challenged Pat to include as many fabrics as possible. Hand appliquéd and quilted. A winner at the Southwest Florida Quilt Festival and NQA, Columbus, OH.

Inspired by A Country Journal pattern by Maggie Walker ©1998.

JULY						
S	M	T	W	T	F	S
					1	2
3	4	5	6	7	8	9
10	11	12	13	14	15	16
17	18	19	20	21	22	23
24	25	26	27	28	29	30
31						

AUGUST

MONDAY
1

TUESDAY
2

WEDNESDAY
3

THURSDAY
4

FRIDAY
5

SATURDAY
6

SUNDAY
7

21ST CENTURY LITTLE GRASS SHACK by Barbara Engelking, Superior, WI, 86" x 100". This quilt was completed entirely by machine with paper piecing to assure accuracy. A delightful swirl of colorful and complex borders consisting of a variety of Log Cabin type designs made this a winner at Pennsylvania National Quilt Extravaganza, Ft. Washington, PA.

Features 20th Century Log Cabin pattern by Claudia Clark Myers/2 Much Fun! ©2003.

			AUGUST			
S	M	T	W	T	F	S
	1	2	3	4	5	6
7	8	9	10	11	12	13
14	15	16	17	18	19	20
21	22	23	24	25	26	27
28	29	30	31			

AUGUST

8

9

10

11

12

13

CAROUSEL
by Mary McLarnon, Mamaroneck, NY, 87" x 87". Inspired by the colors in a children's picture book, Mary adapted the Star of Bethlehem pattern to create her carousel. The original horses were also her idea. Machine pieced and quilted on her forty-year-old sewing machine. Displayed at NQA, Columbus, OH.

14

AUGUST						
S	M	T	W	T	F	S
	1	2	3	4	5	6
7	8	9	10	11	12	13
14	15	16	17	18	19	20
21	22	23	24	25	26	27
28	29	30	31			

AUGUST

MONDAY
15

TUESDAY
16

WEDNESDAY
17

THURSDAY
18

FRIDAY
19

SATURDAY
20

SUNDAY
21

ALBUM FROM PITTSBURGH by Margaret Curley, Pittsburgh, PA, 76" x 76". Margaret's first appliqué quilt includes two original blocks and an original center medallion, with her own layout and border designs. She also added elements to 10 block patterns from Jane Townswick's *Artful Album Quilts* book. Hand appliquéd and hand quilted. Displayed at the Three Rivers Quilt Show, Pittsburgh, PA, NQA, Columbus, and Quilt Festival, Houston.

Features patterns from *Artful Album Quilts* by Jane Townswick, Martingale and Company.

			AUGUST			
S	M	T	W	T	F	S
	1	2	3	4	5	6
7	8	9	10	11	12	13
14	15	16	17	18	19	20
21	22	23	24	25	26	27
28	29	30	31			

AUGUST

MONDAY
22

TUESDAY
23

WEDNESDAY
24

AQS QUILT EXPOSITION, NASHVILLE

THURSDAY
25

AQS QUILT EXPOSITION, NASHVILLE

FRIDAY
26

AQS QUILT EXPOSITION, NASHVILLE

SATURDAY
27

AQS QUILT EXPOSITION, NASHVILLE

KAYAKING THE LAKE SUPERIOR SEA CAVES
by Lynn Gilles, Presque Isle, WI, 39" x 35". This quilt was inspired by photographs of sea caves and cliffs, taken while kayaking in Lake Superior. Lynn experimented by hand painting with dye on background fabric and developed the design using machine appliqué, piecing, and embroidery. It is machine quilted with trees, waves, and rock striations. A winner at A Walk in the North Woods Quilt Show, Eagle River, WI.

SUNDAY
28

			AUGUST			
S	M	T	W	T	F	S
	1	2	3	4	5	6
7	8	9	10	11	12	13
14	15	16	17	18	19	20
21	22	23	24	25	26	27
28	29	30	31			

August/September

MONDAY
29

TUESDAY
30

WEDNESDAY
31

THURSDAY
1

FRIDAY
2

SATURDAY
3

SUNDAY
4

FISH
by Debra Gabel, Clarksville, MD, 62" x 72". The fabric in the center fish was Debra's motivating force for this original fish tale. Metallic threads used for quilting add to the sparkling surface. Machine quilted and appliquéd, paper pieced, and reverse appliquéd. Juried into the AQS Quilt Exposition, Nashville, TN.

			SEPTEMBER			
S	M	T	W	T	F	S
				1	2	3
4	5	6	7	8	9	10
11	12	13	14	15	16	17
18	19	20	21	22	23	24
25	26	27	28	29	30	

SEPTEMBER

MONDAY

5

TUESDAY

6

WEDNESDAY

7

THURSDAY

8

FRIDAY

9

SATURDAY

10

UNIQUE LONE STAR
by Joan Ledanski, Pleasant Prairie, WI, 66" x 66". A pattern from quilt designer Karen Stone is the center of this unusual star quilt. The setting blocks and borders contribute to its difference. All elements were machine done, including the quilting done on Joan's home sewing machine. Colors and patterns allow the illusion that the star floats above an intricate background. A winner at the Wisconsin State Fair, the Kenosha County Fair, and Lighthouse Quilters Guild Show, Racine, WI.

SUNDAY

11

SEPTEMBER						
S	M	T	W	T	F	S
				1	2	3
4	5	6	7	8	9	10
11	12	13	14	15	16	17
18	19	20	21	22	23	24
25	26	27	28	29	30	

SEPTEMBER

<table>
<tr><td>MONDAY
12</td></tr>
<tr><td>TUESDAY
13</td></tr>
<tr><td>WEDNESDAY
14</td></tr>
<tr><td>THURSDAY
15</td></tr>
<tr><td>FRIDAY
16</td></tr>
<tr><td>SATURDAY
17</td></tr>
<tr><td>SUNDAY
18</td></tr>
</table>

THE WEBSTER GARDEN
by Sandi McMillan, Albion, NE, 73" x 83". This is a variation of a Marie Webster pattern. Bright pastels on a dark background set this piece apart from its pastel sisters. Machine appliqué, machine quilting, and machine trapunto were used to create this blue ribbon winner at the Nebraska State Fair, Lincoln, NE.

This is a variation of Marie Webster's 1929 pattern "Gay Garden," from the book *Marie Webster's Garden of Quilts,* by Rosalind Webster Perry and Marty Frolli, published in 2001 by Practical Patchwork.

		SEPTEMBER				
S	M	T	W	T	F	S
				1	2	3
4	5	6	7	8	9	10
11	12	13	14	15	16	17
18	19	20	21	22	23	24
25	26	27	28	29	30	

SEPTEMBER

MONDAY
19

TUESDAY
20

WEDNESDAY
21

THURSDAY FALL EQUINOX
22

FRIDAY
23

SATURDAY
24

SUNDAY
25

SEPTEMBER						
S	M	T	W	T	F	S
				1	2	3
4	5	6	7	8	9	10
11	12	13	14	15	16	17
18	19	20	21	22	23	24
25	26	27	28	29	30	

Red Delicious
Fuji
Golden Delicious
Empire
Cortland
Rome
Gala
Granny Smith
Macoun
Macintosh
Jonagold
Braeburn
October
Tuesday
Wednesday
Thursday
3
4
5
10
11
12
17
18
19
24
25
26
31
Notes:
Notes:

SEPTEMBER/OCTOBER

MONDAY
26

TUESDAY
27

WEDNESDAY
28

THURSDAY
29

FRIDAY
30

SATURDAY
1

SUNDAY
2

OCTOBER

S	M	T	W	T	F	S
						1
2	3	4	5	6	7	8
9	10	11	12	13	14	15
16	17	18	19	20	21	22
23	24	25	26	27	28	29
30	31					

MONDAY
3

TUESDAY   ROSH HASHANAH
4

WEDNESDAY
5

THURSDAY
6

FRIDAY
7

ARBOR LODGE OAKS
by Carol J. Falk, Nebraska City, NE, 50" x 50". With patterns designed from various species of oak leaves found while hiking, Carol made this quilt as a tribute to our national tree. She hand dyed all the leaf fabrics and used machine free-hand appliqué and embroidery to apply the leaves to the background. Machine free-hand quilted. A winner at the Nebraska State Fair and displayed at Heritage Needlework Show, Nebraska City, NE.

SATURDAY
8

SUNDAY
9

OCTOBER

S	M	T	W	T	F	S
						1
2	3	4	5	6	7	8
9	10	11	12	13	14	15
16	17	18	19	20	21	22
23	24	25	26	27	28	29
30	31					

MONDAY COLUMBUS DAY (OBSERVED)
10

TUESDAY
11

WEDNESDAY
12

THURSDAY YOM KIPPUR
13

FRIDAY
14

SATURDAY
15

SEASONS
by Becky Cole, McArthur, OH, 65" x 78". The layout of a cross-stitch panel was the take-off point for this original design. Becky can display this piece as a whole or as four separate units. Machine pieced and appliquéd with thread lace, thread painting, and hand quilting used to bring the designs to life. A winner at the Dogwood Quilt Show, Knoxville, TN, and NQA, Columbus, OH.

SUNDAY
16

OCTOBER

S	M	T	W	T	F	S
						1
2	3	4	5	6	7	8
9	10	11	12	13	14	15
16	17	18	19	20	21	22
23	24	25	26	27	28	29
30	31					

OCTOBER

MONDAY
17

TUESDAY
18

WEDNESDAY
19

THURSDAY
20

FRIDAY
21

SATURDAY
22

AURORA
by Stacie Mann, Lee, ME, 62" x 62". Traditional Fence Rail blocks (paper pieced for accuracy) were used for this complex looking, yet simple piece. Swirling machine embroidery inspired by the Northern Lights was used as surface texture and created a translucent focal point. Displayed at AQS Quilt Exposition, Nashville, TN.

SUNDAY
23

OCTOBER						
S	M	T	W	T	F	S
						1
2	3	4	5	6	7	8
9	10	11	12	13	14	15
16	17	18	19	20	21	22
23	24	25	26	27	28	29
30	31					

OCTOBER

MONDAY
24

TUESDAY
25

WEDNESDAY
26

THURSDAY
27

FRIDAY
28

SATURDAY
29

SUNDAY
30

DAYLIGHT SAVINGS
TIME ENDS

OCTOBER

S	M	T	W	T	F	S
						1
2	3	4	5	6	7	8
9	10	11	12	13	14	15
16	17	18	19	20	21	22
23	24	25	26	27	28	29
30	31					

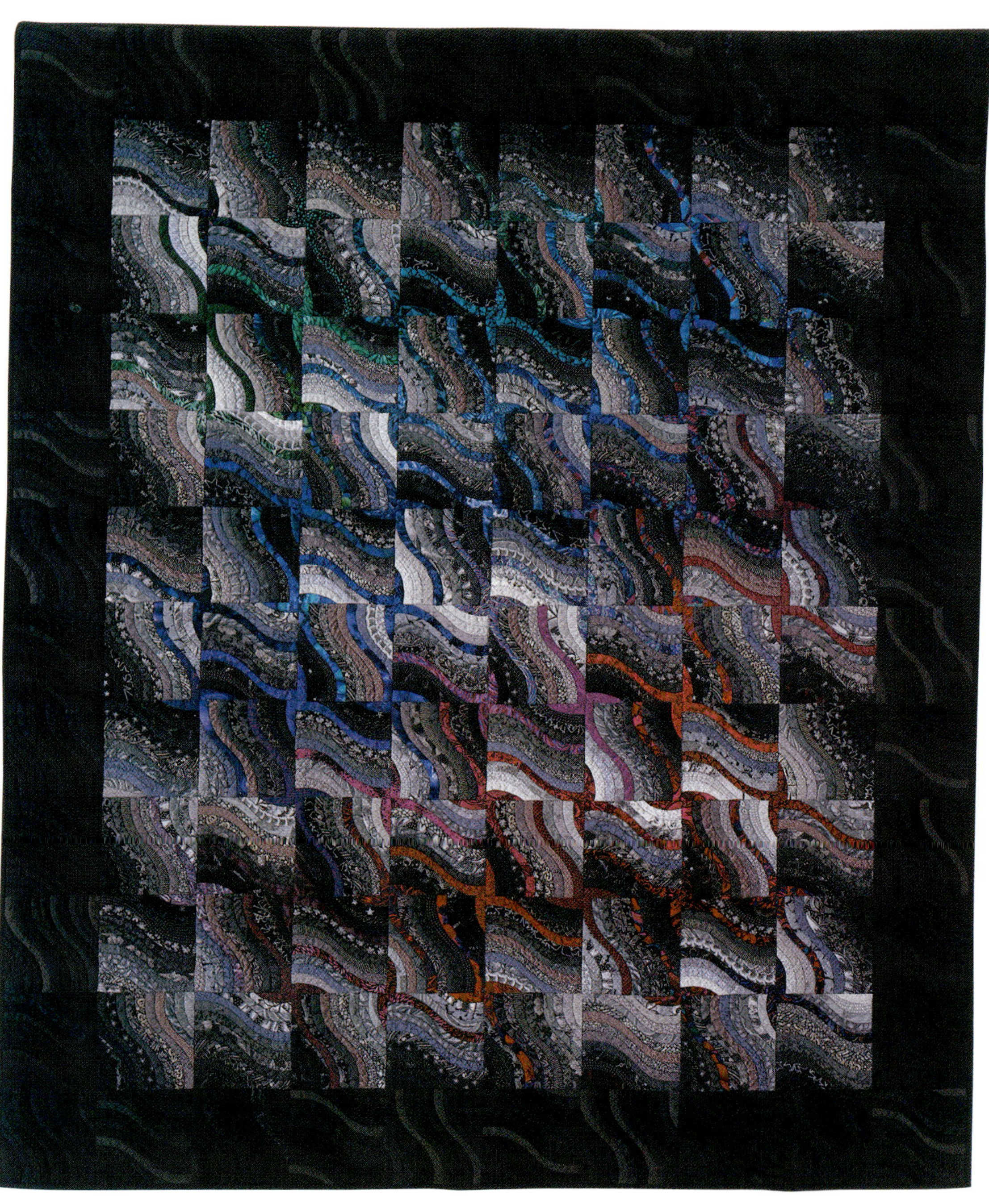

OCTOBER/NOVEMBER

MONDAY HALLOWEEN
31

TUESDAY
1

WEDNESDAY
2

THURSDAY
3

FRIDAY
4

SATURDAY
5

SUNDAY
6

NOVEMBER

S	M	T	W	T	F	S
		1	2	3	4	5
6	7	8	9	10	11	12
13	14	15	16	17	18	19
20	21	22	23	24	25	26
27	28	29	30			

November

MONDAY
7

TUESDAY
8

WEDNESDAY
9

THURSDAY
10

FRIDAY
11   VETERAN'S DAY

SATURDAY
12

SUNDAY
13

RIVERS WEST
by Ann Horton, Redwood Valley, CA, 68" x 59". This quilt celebrates the bicentennial of the Lewis and Clark expedition and has been chosen to be a part of a three-year traveling show to commemorate their travels. The bright yellow star is a pieced block, a C. Stone pattern from the early 1900s called Lewis & Clark. The center is an adaptation of a Charles Russell painting from 1906. Embellished with trade beads, thread painting, ink work, and hand and machine quilting.

NOVEMBER

S	M	T	W	T	F	S
		1	2	3	4	5
6	7	8	9	10	11	12
13	14	15	16	17	18	19
20	21	22	23	24	25	26
27	28	29	30			

NOVEMBER

MONDAY
14

TUESDAY
15

WEDNESDAY
16

THURSDAY
17

FRIDAY
18

SATURDAY
19

SUNDAY
20

COLORADO DREAMIN II
by Mary Richling, Omaha, NE, 32" x 45½". Mary's original design of her log home in Colorado began at a Ruth McDowell retreat. It was duplicated from a photo and a paper pattern was prepared for assembling the top. The pine needles and trees were created from various yarns and threads that were hand stitched to the surface. Machine pieced and quilted. A winner at the Omaha Quilt Guild Quilt Show and the Nebraska State Fair.

			NOVEMBER			
S	M	T	W	T	F	S
		1	2	3	4	5
6	7	8	9	10	11	12
13	14	15	16	17	18	19
20	21	22	23	24	25	26
27	28	29	30			

November

MONDAY
21

TUESDAY
22

WEDNESDAY
23

THURSDAY   THANKSGIVING DAY
24

FRIDAY
25

SATURDAY
26

SUNDAY
27

NOVEMBER						
S	M	T	W	T	F	S
		1	2	3	4	5
6	7	8	9	10	11	12
13	14	15	16	17	18	19
20	21	22	23	24	25	26
27	28	29	30			

November/December

MONDAY
28

TUESDAY
29

WEDNESDAY
30

THURSDAY
1

FRIDAY
2

SATURDAY
3

OLD MUSEUM ROSE
by Chris Kinka, Sturgeon Bay, WI, 87" x 87". This quilt was designed by Muriel Douglas, Oakbrook, IL, and Patti Miller, Elkhorn, WI, from patterns adapted from antique quilts. Chris made this piece by using hand appliqué and piecing. It is hand quilted. A winner at Faithful Circle Quilt Guild Show, Downers Grove, IL, Evergreen Quilt Guild Show, Green Bay, WI, and at Prairie Heritage Quilt Show, Sun Prairie, WI.

SUNDAY
4

DECEMBER

S	M	T	W	T	F	S
				1	2	3
4	5	6	7	8	9	10
11	12	13	14	15	16	17
18	19	20	21	22	23	24
25	26	27	28	29	30	31

December

CATTAILS
by Beth Brady, Marietta, GA, 50" x 46". Raw edge appliqué and great color selection set the stage for the machine quilting that creates the depth and definition for this original piece. All elements converge to convey a sense of peace and serenity at the edge of a forest pond in the evening hours. Displayed at NQA, Charlotte, NC, A Walk in the North Woods, Eagle River, WI, and a winner at Georgia Celebrates Quilts, Marietta, GA.

DECEMBER

S	M	T	W	T	F	S
				1	2	3
4	5	6	7	8	9	10
11	12	13	14	15	16	17
18	19	20	21	22	23	24
25	26	27	28	29	30	31

DECEMBER

MONDAY
12

TUESDAY
13

WEDNESDAY
14

THURSDAY
15

FRIDAY
16

SATURDAY
17

SUNDAY
18

CREATION
by Brenda Brown, Manheim, PA, 66"
x 66". Beads, buttons, and other
embellishments come together with
a colorful palette and innovative layout to form Brenda's version of creation. The center block is an
adaptation of Karen Stone's Unusual
Feather Star paper-piecing pattern.
Machine pieced, hand quilted, beaded, and embellished. Displayed at
Pennsylvania National Quilt Extravaganza, Ft. Washington, PA.

Features adaptation of Unusual Feather Star pattern by Karen Stone.

			DECEMBER			
S	M	T	W	T	F	S
				1	2	3
4	5	6	7	8	9	10
11	12	13	14	15	16	17
18	19	20	21	22	23	24
25	26	27	28	29	30	31

DECEMBER

REMEMBRANCE
by Linda McCuean, New Galilee, PA, 79" x 82". A quilt made by Bertha Stenge in the 1930s called IVY'S PIN-CUSHION was the inspiration for this piece. Linda changed the orientation and border treatment, then added her original quilting designs, requiring more than 105 hours of longarm quilting. Extensive trapunto is shaded by using polar fleece. Machine pieced and appliquéd. A winner at Machine Quilter's Showcase, Springfield, IL, and Pennsylvania National Quilt Extravaganza, Ft. Washington, PA.

			DECEMBER			
S	M	T	W	T	F	S
				1	2	3
4	5	6	7	8	9	10
11	12	13	14	15	16	17
18	19	20	21	22	23	24
25	26	27	28	29	30	31

December/January

TUESDAY
27

WEDNESDAY
28

THURSDAY
29

FRIDAY
30

NIGHT WATCH
by Eunice M. Hill, Rochester, MN, 32" x 37". Eunice's daughter, Becky Dreher, painted a mural including this scene. To duplicate her design, Eunice used hand-dyed fabrics, hand appliqué, machine piecing, and free-hand machine embroidery for the pine branches. Hand quilting emphasizes and brings depth to the other elements. Displayed at Walk in the North Woods, Eagle River, WI, and a ribbon winner at the Olmsted County Fair, Rochester, MN.

SATURDAY
31

SUNDAY
1

NEW YEAR'S DAY

JANUARY						
S	M	T	W	T	F	S
1	2	3	4	5	6	7
8	9	10	11	12	13	14
15	16	17	18	19	20	21
22	23	24	25	26	27	28
29	30	31				

2005

JANUARY

S	M	T	W	T	F	S
						1
2	3	4	5	6	7	8
9	10	11	12	13	14	15
16	17	18	19	20	21	22
23	24	25	26	27	28	29
30	31					

FEBRUARY

S	M	T	W	T	F	S
		1	2	3	4	5
6	7	8	9	10	11	12
13	14	15	16	17	18	19
20	21	22	23	24	25	26
27	28					

MARCH

S	M	T	W	T	F	S
		1	2	3	4	5
6	7	8	9	10	11	12
13	14	15	16	17	18	19
20	21	22	23	24	25	26
27	28	29	30	31		

APRIL

S	M	T	W	T	F	S
					1	2
3	4	5	6	7	8	9
10	11	12	13	14	15	16
17	18	19	20	21	22	23
24	25	26	27	28	29	30

MAY

S	M	T	W	T	F	S
1	2	3	4	5	6	7
8	9	10	11	12	13	14
15	16	17	18	19	20	21
22	23	24	25	26	27	28
29	30	31				

JUNE

S	M	T	W	T	F	S
			1	2	3	4
5	6	7	8	9	10	11
12	13	14	15	16	17	18
19	20	21	22	23	24	25
26	27	28	29	30		

JULY

S	M	T	W	T	F	S
					1	2
3	4	5	6	7	8	9
10	11	12	13	14	15	16
17	18	19	20	21	22	23
24	25	26	27	28	29	30
31						

AUGUST

S	M	T	W	T	F	S
	1	2	3	4	5	6
7	8	9	10	11	12	13
14	15	16	17	18	19	20
21	22	23	24	25	26	27
28	29	30	31			

SEPTEMBER

S	M	T	W	T	F	S
				1	2	3
4	5	6	7	8	9	10
11	12	13	14	15	16	17
18	19	20	21	22	23	24
25	26	27	28	29	30	

OCTOBER

S	M	T	W	T	F	S
						1
2	3	4	5	6	7	8
9	10	11	12	13	14	15
16	17	18	19	20	21	22
23	24	25	26	27	28	29
30	31					

NOVEMBER

S	M	T	W	T	F	S
		1	2	3	4	5
6	7	8	9	10	11	12
13	14	15	16	17	18	19
20	21	22	23	24	25	26
27	28	29	30			

DECEMBER

S	M	T	W	T	F	S
				1	2	3
4	5	6	7	8	9	10
11	12	13	14	15	16	17
18	19	20	21	22	23	24
25	26	27	28	29	30	31

2006

JANUARY

S	M	T	W	T	F	S
1	2	3	4	5	6	7
8	9	10	11	12	13	14
15	16	17	18	19	20	21
22	23	24	25	26	27	28
29	30	31				

FEBRUARY

S	M	T	W	T	F	S
			1	2	3	4
5	6	7	8	9	10	11
12	13	14	15	16	17	18
19	20	21	22	23	24	25
26	27	28				

MARCH

S	M	T	W	T	F	S
			1	2	3	4
5	6	7	8	9	10	11
12	13	14	15	16	17	18
19	20	21	22	23	24	25
26	27	28	29	30	31	

APRIL

S	M	T	W	T	F	S
						1
2	3	4	5	6	7	8
9	10	11	12	13	14	15
16	17	18	19	20	21	22
23	24	25	26	27	28	29
30						

MAY

S	M	T	W	T	F	S
	1	2	3	4	5	6
7	8	9	10	11	12	13
14	15	16	17	18	19	20
21	22	23	24	25	26	27
28	29	30	31			

JUNE

S	M	T	W	T	F	S
				1	2	3
4	5	6	7	8	9	10
11	12	13	14	15	16	17
18	19	20	21	22	23	24
25	26	27	28	29	30	

JULY

S	M	T	W	T	F	S
						1
2	3	4	5	6	7	8
9	10	11	12	13	14	15
16	17	18	19	20	21	22
23	24	25	26	27	28	29
30	31					

AUGUST

S	M	T	W	T	F	S
		1	2	3	4	5
6	7	8	9	10	11	12
13	14	15	16	17	18	19
20	21	22	23	24	25	26
27	28	29	30	31		

SEPTEMBER

S	M	T	W	T	F	S
					1	2
3	4	5	6	7	8	9
10	11	12	13	14	15	16
17	18	19	20	21	22	23
24	25	26	27	28	29	30

OCTOBER

S	M	T	W	T	F	S
1	2	3	4	5	6	7
8	9	10	11	12	13	14
15	16	17	18	19	20	21
22	23	24	25	26	27	28
29	30	31				

NOVEMBER

S	M	T	W	T	F	S
			1	2	3	4
5	6	7	8	9	10	11
12	13	14	15	16	17	18
19	20	21	22	23	24	25
26	27	28	29	30		

DECEMBER

S	M	T	W	T	F	S
					1	2
3	4	5	6	7	8	9
10	11	12	13	14	15	16
17	18	19	20	21	22	23
24	25	26	27	28	29	30
31						

QUILT ART 2005

20 years of beautiful quilts!

Year after year, Klaudeen Hansen and Annette Baker, both of Sun Prairie, WI, have shown you some of the best quilts from across the country. This year is no different. Selecting the quilts for this calendar is becoming more difficult because the quality of work is outstanding.

Klaudeen and Annette enjoy going to different shows to see the best and brightest of the quilt world. They love the fact that they are able to share some of these quilts with you. Hopefully, you will see the same sparkle in these quilts as observed by Klaudeen and Annette.

Klaudeen Hansen
Certified judge
& teacher

Annette Baker
Quilt shop owner

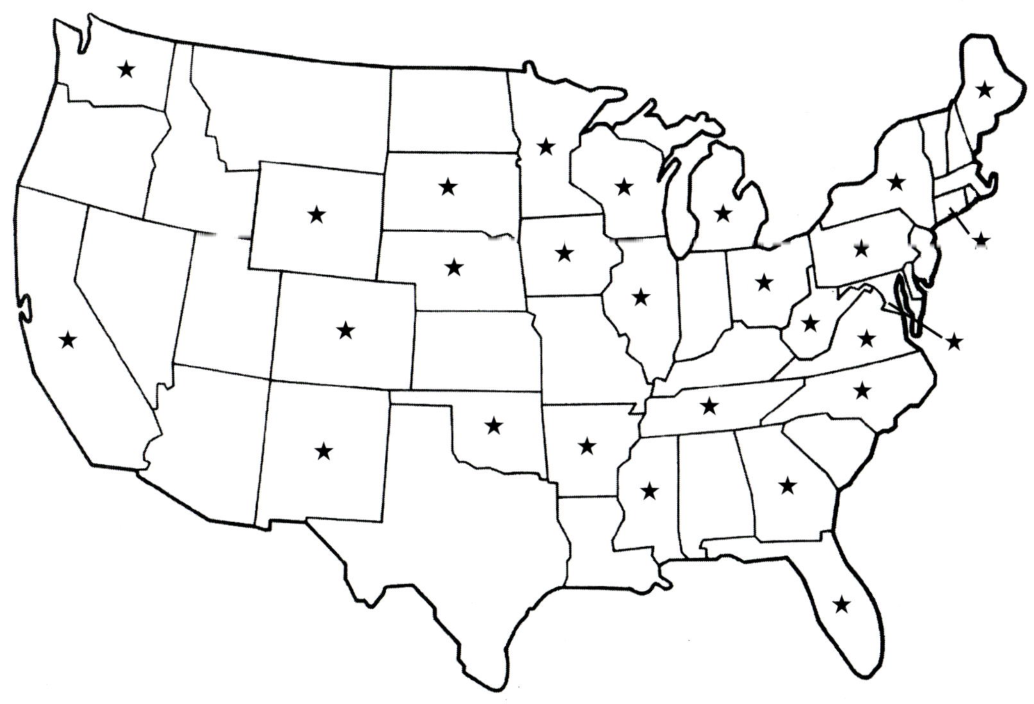

2005 AQS Wall Calendar

Never miss another important event!

Write down every event in this beautiful monthly calendar that features 12 winning quilts from the 2004 AQS Quilt Show & Contest. Each quilt was selected for its superb craftsmanship and beauty. May every month provide you with an inspiration for a new quilt project.

#6420 . . . .$9.95

Additional copies of this calendar may be obtained from your favorite bookseller, sewing center, craft shop, or from

American Quilter's Society
PO Box 3290
Paducah, KY 42002-3290
(270) 898-7903 • fax (270) 898-1173
www.AQSquilt.com
info@AQSquilt.com

@ $12.95 per copy
Add $3.00 to cover postage and handling.

Copyright ©2004 by the American Quilter's Society

All rights reserved. No part of this book may be reproduced, stored in any retrieval system, or transmitted in any form, or by any means including but not limited to electronic, mechanical, photocopy, recording, or otherwise, without the written consent of the publisher.

The publisher has made every effort to ensure the accuracy of information in this calendar but cannot assume liability for any errors.